D1085427

Pebble® Plus

Reptiles

Gila Monsters

by Joanne Mattern

Consulting Editor: Gail Saunders Smith, PhD
Content Consultants: Joe Maierhauser, President/CEO
Terry Phillip, Curator of Reptiles
Reptile Gardens, Rapid City, South Dakota

Capstone press®

Mankato, Minnesota

Pebble Plus is published by Capstone Press,
151 Good Counsel Drive, P.O. Box 669, Mankato, Minnesota 56002.
www.capstonepress.com

Books published by Capstone Press are manufactured with paper
containing at least 10 percent post-consumer waste.

Library of Congress Cataloging-in-Publication Data
Mattern, Joanne, 1963–
  Gila monsters / by Joanne Mattern.
  p. cm. — (Pebble plus. Reptiles)
  Includes bibliographical references and index.
  Summary: "Simple text and photographs present gila monsters, how they look,
where they live, and what they do" — Provided by publisher.
  ISBN 978-1-4296-3323-9 (library binding)
  1. Gila monster — Juvenile literature. I. Title.
QL666.L247.M38 2010
597.95'952 — dc   2009000041

Editorial Credits
Jenny Marks, editor; Matt Bruning, designer; Jo Miller, photo researcher.

Photo Credits
Bruce Coleman Inc./Gary Meszaros, 7; Rod Williams, front cover, Tom Brakefield, 13
Getty Images Inc./Stone/Tim Flach, 9
Nature Picture Library/John Cancalosi, 21
Newscom, 5
Peter Arnold/John Cancalosi, 17
Photo Researchers, Inc/Gerald C. Kelley, 15
Shutterstock/Rusty Dodson, back cover, 1
Visuals Unlimited/Joe & Mary McDonald, 11

Note to Parents and Teachers

The Reptiles series supports science standards related to life science. This book describes and
illustrates Gila monsters. The images support early readers in understanding the text. The
repetition of words and phrases helps early readers learn new words. This book also introduces
early readers to subject-specific vocabulary words, which are defined in the Glossary section.
Early readers may need assistance to read some words and to use the Table of Contents,
Glossary, Read More, Internet Sites, and Index sections of the book.

Table of Contents

Say it like this: HEE-lah MON-ster

A Big Lizard

Gila monsters are
the biggest lizards
in the United States.
From nose to tail, they are
almost 2 feet (.6 meter) long.

These big lizards
have thick, wide bodies.
A Gila monster weighs
from 1 to 3 pounds
(.5 to 1.4 kilograms).

Gila monsters store fat

in their thick tails.

During the winter, Gila monsters

hibernate underground.

They live off the fat until spring.

Watch Out!

Gila monsters have

long claws and sharp teeth.

Claws and teeth help them

hunt and protect themselves.

Gila monsters have

a poisonous bite.

The poison is strong enough

to kill small animals.

Hot Homes

Gila monsters live in deserts.
When it's too hot, they sleep
underground or under rocks.
They come out at night
when it's cooler.

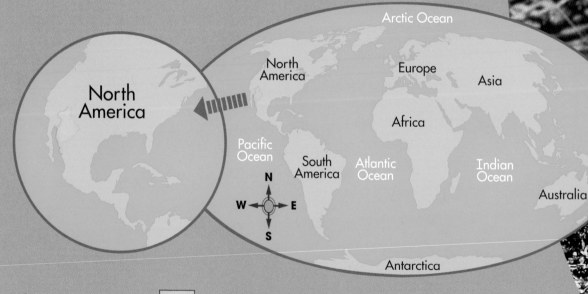

Arctic Ocean

North America

North America

Europe

Asia

Africa

Pacific Ocean

South America

Atlantic Ocean

Indian Ocean

Australia

N
W E
S

Antarctica

where Gila monsters live

Gila monsters hunt

prey at night.

They eat eggs, mice, birds,

frogs, and other lizards.

The Life of a Gila Monster

Female Gila monsters

lay up to 15 eggs.

The eggs hatch in four months.

Gila monsters can live

for more than 20 years.

Gila Monster Life Cycle

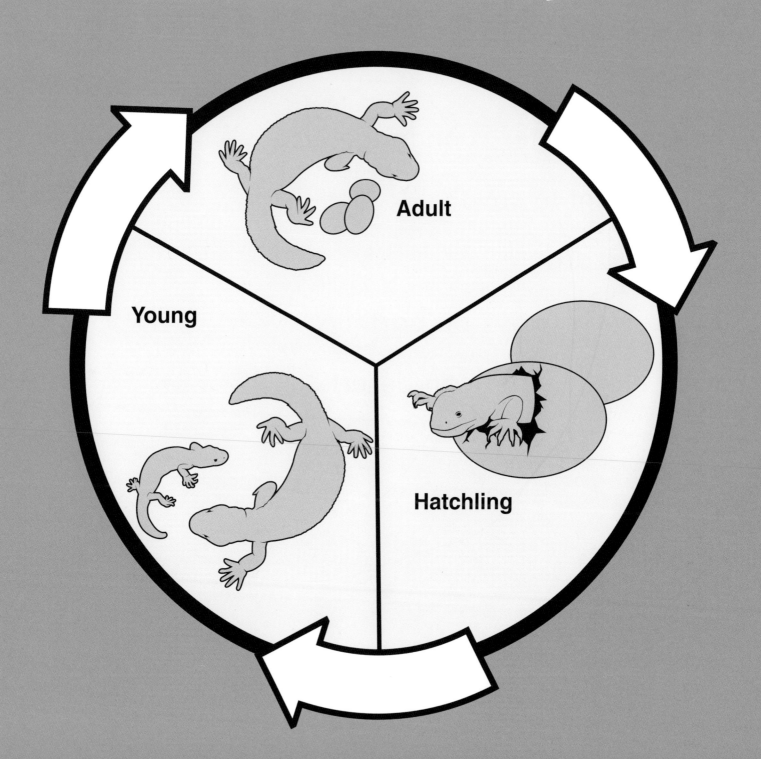

Adult

Young

Hatchling

Saving the Gila Monster

The Gila monster is endangered.

People want to save

this big lizard.

Then it will always be part

of the North American desert.

Glossary

desert — a very dry area of land

endangered — in danger of dying out

hatch — to break out of an egg

hibernate — to spend the winter in a deep sleep

lizard — a reptile with a scaly body and a long tail

poisonous — able to harm or kill with poison or venom

prey — an animal that is eaten by another animal for food

Read More

Macken, JoAnn Early. *Gila Monsters*. Animals that Live in the Desert. Pleasantville, N.Y.: Weekly Reader, 2010.

Mattern, Joanne. *Komodo Dragons*. Reptiles. Mankato, Minn.: Capstone Press, 2010.

Sirota, Lyn A. *Horned Lizards*. Reptiles. Mankato, Minn.: Capstone Press, 2010.

Internet Sites

FactHound offers a safe, fun way to find Internet sites related to this book. All of the sites on FactHound have been researched by our staff.

Here's all you do:

Visit *www.facthound.com*

FactHound will fetch the best sites for you!

Index

Word Count: 180

Grade: 1

Early-Intervention Level: 20